Nelson Mandelamandla

Edited by
Amelia Blossom House
and
Cosmo Pieterse

An Original by Three Continents Press

©Amelia Blossom House & Cosmo Pieterse 1989

An Original by Three Continents Press
1901 Pennsylvania Avenue, N.W.
Washington, D.C. 20006

Library of Congress Cataloging-in-Publication Data:

Nelson Mandelamandla.

    1. Mandela, Nelson, 1918 -   — Poetry.
2. Poetry, Modern—20th century. I. House,
Amelia. II. Pieterse, Cosmo, 1930 - .
PN6110.M24N44 1988 808.81'9351 88-29643
              1989

ISBN 0-89410-644-9
  0-89410-645-7 (pbk.)

Cover Art ©1989 Fran Blumenstein

Illustrations by Robert Douglas, Feni Dumile, and Selma Waldman.
©Three Continents Press 1989

Pity for our conquerors, omniscient and naive! . . .

Death traces a shining circle
above this man,
gently sprinkling stars about his head.
Death breathes like a mad thing
in the ripe roughness of his arms.
Death gallops in the prison like a white
horse.
Death gleams in the darkness
like a cat's eyes.
Death hiccups
like the water under coral reefs.
Death is a wounded bird.
Death wanes,
wavers.
Death is a great shady tree.
Death expires in a white
pool of silence.

Puffs of night
at the four corners
of this dawn.
Convulsions of stiffening
death.
Tenacious destiny.
Will the splendor
of this blood
not burst mute earth
with its upright cries?

Excerpt from "Notes on a Return to the Native Land"
by Aimé Césaire
(trans. E.C.K.)

Acknowledgments

The editors and Three Continents Press wish to thank all the contributors for their messages and poems; we have permission to publish the material in this volume, but copyright of individual poems remains with each poet.

Where works may previously have been published, we have the author's permission to reprint in this "birthday" volume; we acknowledge these poets and their publishers, who, of course, retain individual copyright. Reprints, that we are aware of, are poems by:

Margaret Alexander, Margaret Burroughs, Abena Busia, Wilfred Cartey, Golden, Lenrie Peters, Margaret Walker; also: Don Mattera from *Azanian Love Song*, (Skotaville Publishers, Johannesburg), and the excerpts from an abridged version of the *Cahier D'un Retour Au Pays Natal*, published under the title *Notes on a Return to the Native Land* in *The Negritude Poets: An Anthology of Translations from the French* (Viking Press, New York, 1975), reprinted here with permission of the editor and translator, Ellen Conroy Kennedy. For the original permission to translate this version of Aimé Césaire's great poem (©1956 Présence Africaine, Paris), the editor-translator is grateful to Présence Africaine.

88/9 DUMILE.

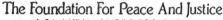

The Foundation For Peace And Justice

An Extended Ministry of the Bellville N.G. Sending Kerk

TEL: (021) 951-2178
TELEX 5-22381

P.O. BOX 316
KASSELSVLEI 7533
SOUTH AFRICA

FROM: Dr Allan Boesak's Office - S.A.
DATE: 31 August 1988

NELSON MANDELA MEANS MANY THINGS TO MANY PEOPLE. FOR THE GOVERNMENTS OF THE WORLD, HE IS AN INESCAPABLE POINT ON EVERY AGENDA CONCERNING SOUTH AFRICA AND THE FUTURE OF THIS TROUBLED, TRAGIC, BELOVED LAND. TO THE SOUTH AFRICAN GOVERNMENT, HE IS WHAT IS STRANGELY CALLED A DILEMMA, A TERRORIST, A PRISONER WHO DESERVES TO BE WHERE HE IS. FOR US, THE OPPRESSED PEOPLE OF SOUTH AFRICA, HE IS A FATHER AND A LEADER, A SYMBOL OF COURAGE AND HOPE. FOR FORTY YEARS THE NATIONALIST GOVERNMENT HAS BEEN IN POWER. FOR US THIS HAS BEEN FORTY YEARS OF SUFFERING, FORCED REMOVALS, INTIMIDATION AND MURDER. WE HAVE SEEN OUR LAND ROBBED, OUR ORGANIZATIONS BANNED, OUR PEOPLE BANISHED, OUR LEADERS IMPRISONED AND EXILED, OUR CHILDREN DIE.

WE HAVE BEEN LIVING IN CHAINS, BUT IN A VERY REAL SENSE WE ARE MORE FREE THAN THOSE WHO HAVE HELD US HOSTAGE FOR SO LONG NOW. AND IN THIS TOO, MANDELA HAS BECOME A SYMBOL. LANGUISHING IN JAIL FOR 26 YEARS, HE HAS NONETHELESS CAPTURED THE IMAGINATION OF THE WORLD AND THE UNDISPUTED REVERENCE OF A WHOLE NATION. FOR ALL OF THEIR POWER, THE SOUTH AFRICAN GOVERNMENT ARE AFRAID OF HIM. BEING IN PRISON, HE HAS HAD THE ESSENTIAL FREEDOM, THE AMAZING COURAGE TO REFUSE CONDITIONAL RELEASE, UNDERSTANDING, EVEN NOW, THAT HIS FREEDOM IS INEXTRICABLY BOUND TO THE FREEDOM OF HIS PEOPLE. IT IS THE GOVERNMENT, NOT HE, WHO ARE LIVING IN THE HOUSE OF FEAR, KNOWING THAT THEIR FALSE GODS OF LIES AND PROPAGANDA, OF GUNS AND CASSPIRS, OF TANKS AND NUCLEAR BOMBS WILL IN THE END NOT DELIVER THEM. NELSON MANDELA IS FREE BECAUSE HE DOES NOT HAVE TO FEAR TOMORROW. P W BOTHA KNOWS

The Foundation For Peace And Justice

An Extended Ministry of the Bellville N.G. Sending Kerk

TEL: (021) 951-2178
TELEX S-22321

P O BOX 315
KASSELSVLEI 7533
SOUTH AFRICA

MANDELA REPRESENTS THE JUST STRUGGLE OF HIS PEOPLE, THEIR DETERMINATION TO WIN THIS BATTLE. P W BOTHA IS PRESIDING OVER THE DEATH OF A POLICY CONCEIVED IN HELL.

THE POEMS IN THIS MARVELLOUSLY CAPTIVATING VOLUME REFLECT ALL THIS: OUR ANGER AT THE CRIME OF KEEPING A MAN OF SUCH STATURE IN PRISON; OUR REJECTION OF THE PROPAGANDA DISMISSING THE MAN AND HIS ORGANIZATION AS TERRORIST; OUR UNDERSTANDING, THROUGH OUR DAILY SUFFERING OF THE MOTIVATIONS WHICH LED MANDELA AND OTHER IMPRISONED AND EXILED LEADERS TO EMBARK ON AN ARMED STRUGGLE. THEY REFLECT OUR HOPE AND OUR CERTAINTY THAT MANDELA SHALL BE FREE AND WITH HIM ALL OTHER POLITICAL PRISONERS. WE KNOW THE DAY WILL COME THAT THEY SHALL BE REUNITED WITH THEIR FAMILIES AND THEIR PEOPLE, TO MAKE A CONTRIBUTION TO THE CREATION OF A S.A. WHERE OUR PEOPLE WILL NO LONGER DIE ON THE STREETS OF OUR NATION, BUT WILL LIVE IN PEACE AND JUSTICE. THIS IS WHAT WE WORK FOR.

GOD BLESS AFRICA
GUIDE HER RULERS
BLESS HER CHILDREN
GIVE HER PEACE.

ALLAN A BOESAK

GOD BLESS AFRICA
GUIDE HER RULERS
BLESS HER CHILDREN
GIVE HER PEACE.

ALLAN A BOESAK

vii

Table Of Contents

Illustrations

Part I

Children's Poems

And here at the end of dawn is my virile prayer,
Eyes fixed on the beautiful city I prophesy:
May I hear neither laughter nor cries,
Give me the sorcerer's wild faith,
Give to my hands the power to mold,
Give to my soul the temper of steel,
I do not shrink. Make of my head a spearhead, and of my self, my heart,
make not a father nor a brother but the father, brother, son; not a husband,
but the lover of this single people;
Make me rebel against all vanity but as docile to its genius,
As the fist is to the arm;
Make me the servant of its blood,
The trustee of its resentment,
Make of me a man who terminates,
Make of me a man who initiates,
Make of me a man who contemplates,
But make of me as well a man who sows;
Make me the executor of these lofty works,
For now is the time to gird one's loins like a valiant man.

But in doing so, my heart, preserve me from all hatred,
Make not of me that man of hate
For whom I've only hate,
For to allot myself
This single race
You know my love to be tyrannical,
You know that it is not from hate
For other races
That I seek to be the plowman
Of this single race,
You know that what I wish
For the universal hunger,
For the universal thirst,
Is to shake it free at last,
To summon from its inner depths
The succulence of fruit.

Excerpt from "Notes on a Return to the Native Land"
by Aimé Césaire
(trans. E.C.K.)

3

My country   (for Mandela)

I stand by the gate
School's out
Smoke fills the location
Tears come to my eyes

I wipe them away
I walk into the kitchen
To see my mother's
Black hard-washing hands
A forceful smile from
A tired face

We sit and have supper
I pick up a picture of
My father and look
My mother turns away
Tries to hide

My father left my mother
In his arms
He is roughly separated
From her

The van pulls away
Mother watches bravely enough
I as a child do
Not understand

My heart aches
How I long to see my father
At least to hold his hand
And comfort him
Or at least to tell him
He'll be back some day.

—Zinziswa Mandela
(*at the age of twelve years*)

4

Africa

Africa is a lovely continent,
But in it you will not find
People laughing but
You will always find
Our tears flowing
Our tears full of blood
Men and women
Heroes of our land.

We feel for our land
We need power and
Peace and friendship
We feel for our children
Who have been arrested
Who have fallen underground
Fallen for their land.

Let's all together fall for one
and one will fall for all
Let's all together take up
Our revolutionary fight.

—Ronald Chambale (16)

Soweto Pains

Influx control
Pass laws
Chains!
Chains in our hands

Die Boere kan mos nie hoor
We don't want them
Rivulets of people
Paving their way
In the steel sand of Soweto
Exploded fascist arrogance
With bonfires of dompass.

Soweto! Soweto!
Blood, blood, bl-oo-od!
Suffering!
Pain!
Racist troops mowing my people down
Rows like cabbages lying
Rows of heads of men
Maimed for their aspirations
Sharp razors cutting
Cutting through the truth
Waterfalls of blood
For People's Power.
Here we come
To kill injustice
Here we come
To avenge those
Streams of blood
And make you
A living symbol
Of our times.

George Maleka (14)

June 16th 1976

On that day, June 16th 1976,
It was that day
When children and students
Were for striking against the Boers.
They were walking in the streets
Singing
"Down with Apartheid"
The slogans say.

They were going, telling people
They must not go to work
Telling people they must meet
In the big stadium.

When they were meeting
The police fired
Teargas and bullets
The people had stones against guns

There was a young boy
Called Hector Peterson
He was 13 years old
Shot by the police
Young Hector Peterson
Bled to death.

His mother cried as she lingered
On the street of death
And said "Power to the People"
Let us continue with the struggle
We. shall win!

Ida Glrenda Sithole (14)

7

Black Child

Black child
No king is greater than your father
No woman is welcome like your mother
No nurse is kinder than your sister
No fighter is braver than your brother.

The road to freedom is tough
The way to a new home is rough

Day will pass
Time will come
When we will walk
Through the tough road
To freedom.

Nana Masasu (14)

Echoes That Shiver the Sky

I emerge by the front door
Confronting all my miseries
All I can hear is the voice
That echoes and shivers the sky.
Down the road I can hear the people
Shouting for a better education.
It was a peaceful demonstration,
Then I heard the sound of a bullet.
It made the people angry
And I heard the scream that
Echoed, echoed and shivered the sky.

It was bullets and a gun of a white man
In the black man's hand
Giving death to Hector Peterson and his comrades.
The streets were made into battlefields
With their racist guns in hand
They could feel the fire of joy.
For I would be one with many
Whose tears I must drain
Draining with the echoes that
Filled the sky
Echoes that shiver the sky.

Sandile Dube (14)

The Tears in Africa

Tears in our country
Why? Why? Tears in our country.
Haag man, haag man. Why?
Why you white people, you rule in our country?

Why? Why? Man, our country is like this?
You just remember that day
My brothers and sisters, friends,
Death on the dusty street, blood flowing
On the street like water flowing.

Haag man, haag man, let's remember
All our people that the Boers have killed
Haag man. The Boers, Tears, Bullets
Can never stop us
Going to Freedom.

Thabo Serote (15)

Peace

Let's build a wall of peace,
I'm not satisfied with this little peace of Mazimbu
We need peace in our own country
We will never be satisfied by the peace of exile

We will be satisfied when freedom comes
When we will be finding ourselves in our own country

On the day that South Africa will be finding only peace

Freedom is needed
Peace is needed
Peace high and low
Freedom day and night.

Molly Khanyile (17)

Part II

Supporting Letters

Look, I am nothing but a man,
No degradation, no spit disturbs me.
I am nothing but a man who no longer accepts
being angry
Who has nothing in his heart any more
But a burning immensity of love.

Excerpt from "Notes on a Return to the Native Land"

by Aimé Césaire
(trans. E.C.K.)

FROM THE ANGLICAN ARCHBISHOP OF CAPE TOWN

The Most Reverend Desmond M. Tutu, D.D. F.K.C.

BISHOPSCOURT CLAREMONT CAPE 7700

TELEPHONE: (021) 71-2531
FAX: (021) 71-4193
TELEX: 524320 CPSA

10 August 1988

Iron bars cannot contain a spirit. Iron bars cannot suppress hope. Iron bars may restrict freedom but they cannot stop men and women yearning to be free. Although Nelson Mandela has been separated from his people we know that his spirit, his hope and his passionate desire for his people to be free in a new South Africa is with us.

In this year of his 70th birthday there is not much to celebrate in South Africa. Apartheid continues to impoverish the lives of millions of people. It is a country in the midst of an unproclaimed war against its own citizens. But we rejoice in the certainty that justice and righteousness will overcome evil and oppression and we shall all be free, black and white together.

+Desmond Cape Town

"Beloved, let us love one another, for love is of God — if there is this love among you,
then all will know that you are my disciples."

AFRICA NETWORK
Resources Information Action • P.O. Box 5366 Evanston, IL 60204

Chairman
Dennis Brutus
Vice-Chairpersons
Jan Carew
Joy Carew
Nancy Singham
Secretary/Treasurer
Y.B. Holly

Educational Outreach
Coordinator
Mokubung Nkomo
Washington D.C.
Coordinator
Allan Ebert

Educational Outreach
Representatives
Nomonde Ngubo
(Washington D.C.)
Winston Nagan
(Florida)
Ruth Andris
Stuart McCarrell
Sterling Plumpp
(Illinois)
Vernon Domingo
(Massachusetts)
Martha Page Blunt
Don Cooney
Leander Jones
Don van Hoven
(Michigan)
Winsome Munro
Elizabeth Schmidt
(Minnesota)
Vera Michelson
(New York)
Margaret Lee
(Tennessee)
Hal Wylie
(Texas)
John Dommisse
(Virginia)
Peter Bonmer
Gail Tremblay
Selma Waldman
(Washington)
Covenant Against
Apartheid at Home
& Abroad/Clergy &
Laity Concerned
(New York, NY)
Young Socialist
Alliance
(New York, NY)
Capital District Against
Apartheid & Racism
(Albany, NY)

June, 1988

I am glad to join in greeting Nelson Mandela on his 70th Birthday and in paying tribute to his heroic struggle for Justice in South Africa - for this he has endured prison for 25 years.

I recall seeing Nelson on Robben Island shortly before I left there: we were kept in the maximum security section and had broken stones together there: he was strong and unbowed: firm in his commitment to struggle and freedom:

I recall the quiet dignity and confidence which he showed when he spoke of the day when our country would be free.

We salute his courage and we honor him by renewing our own commitment to the ongoing battle for a free South Africa.

Fraternally
Dennis Brutus
Africa Network

14

United States Senate

COMMITTEE ON
AGRICULTURE, NUTRITION, AND FORESTRY
WASHINGTON, DC 20510-6000

July 12, 1988

Mr. Nelson Mandela
c/o Africa Network
Resources Information Action
Evanston, Illinois

Dear Mr. Mandela:

It has just come to my attention that you will soon be
celebrating your 70th birthday. Please let me take this
opportunity to extend my very best wishes on this special
occasion.

You have seem many moments of our society's history unfold
before you. The many tribulations you have experienced have
added pages to our text books. I must extend my deepest
appreciation and gratitude for your devotion to your people and
their needs.

Again, please accept my very best wishes to you as you celebrate
this special day, and my special prayers for your success and
happiness.

Sincerely,

MITCH McCONNELL
UNITED STATES SENATOR

MM/nlw

To Nelson Mandela-

     The struggle for jobs, peace and equality in this country
is part of the struggle to free Nelson Mandela and the South
African people. Our common struggle against oppression can only
end in victory. Your example continues to give us courage to
carry on the fight here. Victory!

                              Nancy Singham
                              Vice-chairperson
                              Africa Network

15

United States Senate
WASHINGTON, DC 20510

July 1, 1988

Ms. Amelia Blossom House
Coordinator
Nelson Mandela Publication
  Project
P.O. Box 1222
New Gardens
Fort Knox, Kentucky 40121

Dear Ms. House:

Thank you for letting me know of the Africa Network project to
publish a Tribute to Nelson Mandela.

With the help of committed and resourceful people, such as
you and those working within the Africa Network, we will be
able to help the people of South Africa in their struggle for
freedom and justice.

My best wishes.

Cordially,

Paul Simon
United States Senator

PS/lo

230 S. DEARBORN
KLUCZYNSKI BLDG., 38TH FLOOR
CHICAGO, IL 60604
312/353-4952

3 WEST OLD CAPITOL PLAZA
SUITE 1
SPRINGFIELD, IL 62701
217/492-4960

8787 STATE ST.
SUITE 212
EAST ST. LOUIS, IL 62203
618/398-7707

250 WEST CHERRY
ROOM 115-B
CARBONDALE, IL 62901
618/457-3653

CHARLES B. RANGEL
16TH CONGRESSIONAL DISTRICT
NEW YORK

DEPUTY WHIP

COMMITTEES:
WAYS AND MEANS

CHAIRMAN, SUBCOMMITTEE ON
SELECT REVENUE MEASURES

SUBCOMMITTEE ON HEALTH

CHAIRMAN, SELECT COMMITTEE ON
NARCOTICS ABUSE AND CONTROL

GEORGE A. DALLEY
COUNSEL AND STAFF DIRECTOR

Congress of the United States
House of Representatives
Washington, DC 20515

☐ 2330 RAYBURN HOUSE OFFICE BUILDING
WASHINGTON, DC 20515
TELEPHONE: (202) 225-4365

DISTRICT OFFICES
MS. VIVIAN E. JONES
DISTRICT ADMINISTRATOR

☐ 163 WEST 125TH STREET
NEW YORK, NY 10027
TELEPHONE: (212) 663-3900

☐ 656 WEST 181ST STREET
NEW YORK, NY 10033
TELEPHONE: (212) 927-5333

☐ 2112 SECOND AVENUE
NEW YORK, NY 10029
TELEPHONE: (212) 348-9630

PLEASE RESPOND TO
OFFICE CHECKED

JULY 18, 1988

It is with great respect and admiration that
I send my warmest greetings to you, Mr.
Mandela, on the occasion of your seventieth
birthday. Your relentless courage has been an
inspiration to all of us that believe in
freedom and justice for all people regardless
of race and color.

It has been in the spirit of human rights and
freedom, that I as a United States
Congressman, have supported legislation to
free the Black South African people from the
tyrannous rule of apartheid. Undoubtedly, any
progress that is made in the pursuit of human
rights is always in part a tribute to Nelson
Mandela.

Mr Mandela you have my support, and that of
many of my constituents, a largely Black
community in Harlem, New York. On behalf of
all of us I wish you the very best in your
struggle against oppression.

Sincerely,

CHARLES B. RANGEL
Member of Congress

17

MIKE LOWRY
SEVENTH DISTRICT
WASHINGTON

2454 RAYBURN HOUSE OFFICE BUILDING
WASHINGTON, DC 20515
(202) 225-3106

318 FIRST AVENUE SOUTH #300
SEATTLE, WA 98104
(206) 442-7170

Congress of the United States
House of Representatives
Washington, DC 20515

COMMITTEES
BUDGET
MERCHANT MARINE AND FISHERIES
BANKING, FINANCE AND URBAN
AFFAIRS
(ON LEAVE)

September 6, 1988

Dear Mr. Mandela:

Your 70th birthday is a cause for celebration for the people of South Africa. Although the occasion would be far more joyous if you were celebrating it as a free man, your spirit as well as your resolve that South Africa must be free has in many ways freed you in the hearts and minds of your people and other freedom-loving people around the world.

South Africa is a vibrant nation, exceedingly rich in natural and human resources. But for far too long the blight of apartheid has colored the nation's horizons. Discrimination, oppression, violence, and the haunting knowledge that one is despised in one's own land is the reality for more than 24 million black South Africans. This situation cannot continue for long. Despite the South African government's actions closing off virtually all means of peaceful protest, change will come.

I have been working with other concerned members of Congress for years to develop a U.S. foreign policy that will help to bring about peaceful, non-violent change in South Africa, to heal the nation's wounds, and to establish a non-racial, democratic society in which all people are equal under the letter and spirit of the law. I am continuing these efforts.

I join all freedom-loving people throughout the world in wishing you a happy 70th birthday.and continuing our commitment to help end apartheid. We also hope that your 71st birthday will be spent as a free man in a free South Africa.

Sincerely,

Mike Lowry
Member of Congress

18

500 EAST 62ND STREET • NEW YORK, NEW YORK 10021

national urban league

OFFICE OF THE PRESIDENT
& CHIEF EXECUTIVE OFFICER

July 15, 1988

Ms. Amelia Blossom House
P.O. Box 1222
New Gardens
Fort Knox, KY 40121

Dear Ms. House:

The seventieth birthday of Nelson Mandela is a time for all of us
to reaffirm our commitment to the struggle for human rights.

Today, Nelson Mandela remains imprisoned twenty-five years after
leading the fight against apartheid for oppressed South Africans.
South Africa is still aflame with spontaneous, grass-roots revolt
against a white supremacist system that relegates eighty-five per-
cent of the population to brutalizing oppression.

We in America know all too well the horrors of oppression, slavery
and the immoral legacy of racism that now exists.

The ideals and principles that Nelson Mandela believed in twenty-five
years ago have proved as indomitable as his spirit. We continue to
support his and our great cause; we stand united in our common fight
for equality and righteousness.

Sincerely,

John E. Jacob
President and Chief
  Executive Officer

19

Part III

Poems

And I tell myself Bordeaux and Nantes and Liverpool and New York
and San Francisco,
there is no place on this earth without my fingerprint,
and my heel upon the skeleton of skyscrapers, and my
sweat in the brilliance of diamonds!
Who can boast of more than I?
Virginia   Tennessee   Georgia   Alabama
Monstrous putrefactions of inoperative
revolts,
swamps of putrid blood,
trumpets absurdly stopped,
red lands, sanguine,
consanguine.

This is mine too: a little
cell in the Jura Mountains,
a little cell,
the snow lines its bars with white,
the snow is white
jailer standing guard before a prison.
This is mine,
a man alone
imprisoned in white,
a man alone who defies the white
cries of white
death
(TOUSSAINT, TOUSSAINT
L'OUVERTURE),
a man who fascinates the white
hawk of white
death,
a man alone in a sterile sea of white
snow,

Excerpt from "Notes on a Return to the Native Land"
by Aimé Césaire
(trans. E.C.K.)

22

Father to Son

Father
Yes, Son
Who is Nelson Mandela?
He is many things to many people, my son
He is a—
man
husband
father
leader
fighter

Father
Yes, Son
Why did they put Mr. Mandela in jail for such a long time?
For many reasons, my son
He is a—
black man
devoted husband
loving father
nation's leader
apartheid fighter

Father
Yes, Son
What is Apartheid?
It is the white South African's system of oppressing the black
South African majority, my son
Apartheid does not allow—
black men political rights
devoted husbands to live with their families
loving fathers to raise their children in equality
national leaders to speak the truth
freedom fighters the right to struggle against tyranny

Father
Yes, Son
Will Nelson Mandela ever be free?
That is a difficult question, my son
However even in prison—
black men continue to demand liberty
devoted husbands cherish their wives
loving fathers are symbols of strength and pride
national leaders command the spirit and direction of the people
freedom fighters strike fear in the hearts and minds of their
oppressors

Father
Yes, Son
How soon will apartheid end?
Soon, very soon, my son

J.L. Adams
Joliet, Illinois
July 7, 1988

Honor: Our Story Into This History

I. Survival Motion

(In honor of Winnie and Nelson Mandela)

What am I,
If not survival motion?
The Black Woman
Of Boundless Burdens
Of a Bound Man,
What am I?...
If not our
Freedom?

II. Children of Rage

Behind
barbed wire
and broken window
pains,
we clutch
the sides of
metal and mortar
of hunger and isolation, of mettle

we clutch
the empty spaces
where our fathers
stood
near our mothers
and us
near our grandparents
and us
near our uncles
and aunts
near our cousins
and our sisters
our brothers
near our communities
and us.

Before
they were
swallowed
by factories and mines
by lynch mobs
and Robben Islands
by forced employment
and unemployment
each death by cruel death.

But
we warm
the empty spaces
with the memory
of our fathers' souls
with the heat
of our youth
and our anger
as we hurl
the scattered lives
that lay about
our feet
at guns
at tear gas
at tanks
as we hurl
the bricks of our determination
and the bottles of our anger
to destroy
the walls between
our fathers and ourselves.

Behind
the daybreaks
and clear mornings
we watch
our Nanas
and our Mamas
gather dust and concrete
between their toes
as we clutch
the sides of
closing doors
and empty tables
of our anger and our love.

Behind
the cold cereal
and ground meal
and dust
we watch
the oats boil
and the bacon sizzle
as our nostrils
fill with
others' greed and contempt
and the eyes of
our Nanas and our Mamas
fill the corners
of other homes
and other kitchens
as we clutch
the hot sides
of loneliness and hunger
as we clutch
Rage.

We are
children of the night
whose days
are stolen legacies
of blood knots
massacred and maimed
lynched and banned
to a world
of Robben Islands.

We are
the children of
Birmingham and Soweto
who watch
our fathers
dangle in Mississippi woods
and languish in Johannesburg jails.

We are
children of rage
orphaned
by greed
and barbarism
starved
between
granaries and grasslands.

We are
children of Fanon
waging an incomplete war
upon ourselves
our rage
and anguish
and pain
glazed by
opportunism
and contempt for our lives.

We are
children of the tempest
tossed rudely
upon reddened seas
of this world
our roots
crudely severed.

We are
children of rage
and retribution
our severed bonds
others mistake
for our age
now roots our legacy
and our charred
abandoned fathers
and our abused

maligned mothers
are the images
that nurture us through the nights
and lead us through the days.

We are
children of generations
of destruction and rape
of dope and destitution
of hope and humanity
our rage
fuels us....

for fullness
for freedom!

Diedre L. Badejo
Kingston, Rhode Island
May 28, 1987

A Birthday in the Dust

For Mandela in his Seventies

The dust and great trees
Mark the contrast,
Brown sediment settles
Over ripe savannahs,
Lush growth bounds its space.
Dust is an itinerant reminder
Of soil possessed.
Its element is wind,
Rustling trees,
Carrying fine grains everywhere.

Forests of Johannesburg are a
Rich burgeoning of stone and steel,
White settlers are lush,
Reducing black and brown life
To the invisible,
Wind, riding out of bantustans and urban bistros,
Blows majestic clouds
Like prophecies of change.

Speckles are what you catch,
Nelson Mandela,
In the sunlit stream of your cell;
A swirl of brown and black that reminds you
Of the day the earth was born,
Cosmic matter that will not abate.
You are a grain no bounded moment can contain,
No great and settled trees
Resist.

Houston A. Baker, Jr.
Centre Square, Pennsylvania

Black Litany

You can't be the Devil
   unless you're
      truly evil
      ultimate evil
      real evil
      actual evil

   Witness our world
   Controlled by the Devil

LIES & MURDER
ARE HOLY UN
HATE PAYS
IGNORANCE
POWERFUL!

HUMANITY ENDANGERED
   ITS FUTURE
      EXISTENCE
      UNCERTAIN

Evil is Stronger Than Good
   God
   Is a Slave!

THE DEVIL IS RULER OF EVERYTHING

EVIL IS SUPREME!

So *this* is what
Hell
is
!

Amiri Baraka
New York, New York

(Song for...)
Winnie Mandela—Beloved Heroine

(Chant)
NOMZAMO
Winnie Mandela
Beloved Heroine
Spirited Soldier
Life on the Line
Mother of the Nation
See her Lovelight
Shine
Mother of the Nation
See her Lovelight
Shine
Winnie Mandela.

Beautiful and brave
is she,
A symbol of Courage
To All
Who strive to be free.
We love her Grace
and Dignity;
Beloved Heroine
is she—
Winnie Mandela.

Spirited Soldier
Life on the Line
She leads the way
Never showing
Doubts and Fears
Soft gentle Eyes
Reflecting all
Those unshed Tears.

32

The endless days, the lonely nights,
   All filled with TENDER
      memories
      of Him
   and their Great Love
   that she holds dear
Together, though torn apart
She carries, Deep, within her heart
His Dream, Her Dream, Their vision
   Peace and Freedom
      For us All.
   Peace and Freedom
      For us All

(*End with chant*)

Sathima Bea Benjamin
New York, New York
September 1987

Abafazi (Women)

In Memoriam: Dulcie September, representative of the African National
Congress in Europe, killed in her Paris office by fascist agents on March 29,
1988

Where the shining Tyumie River
winds down through the sunlit
Amatola mountains, blue—
shadowed in their distances
along the banks stand miles
of waving corn, the blade-shaped
leaves flashing as the wind rustles
through them and they throw back
the shafts of light that fall on them:

the trees stand tall, aloof and dreaming in
the haze of the warm midday heat
except for the young blue spruces—
they seem alive and restless with magic
and a blue shade, as if moonlight
lingers there, is gathered around them.
Through these valleys and mountain slopes
warriors once poured down to defend
their land and fought and gave their lives:
their rich blood ran thick and slow
and shining as they died, they poured
their blood with their fierce unrelenting anger
into this rich dark fertile soil:
and the men and women fight on
and give their lives:
the struggle continues.

For Dulcie September, Ruth First, and all the heroic fighting women of
South Africa.

Dennis Brutus
Pittsburgh, Pennsylvania

Word & World

I. Genesis 4:3-10

"Am I my brother's keeper?"
first breaking of the blood bond;
reluctant question to a question of earth-blood—
Not guilt imposed, but recognitions;
source of first responsibilities—
Love half given;
fruitless offerings ill-received.
And the voice that asks the questions
Is the self that knows the answer.

II.

The histories of nations
are in the end spelt out
only through the dying breaths
of succeeding generations.

And of those now laboring to be born,
the first of these generations must weep
and bear a heavy burden
from age to hopeless age on age
that the children's children's
embittered children
may at the last first learn
to laugh, among the ripening fruits
they with silent tears now sow.

Abena P.A. Busia

Tshaka Zulu to Today's Freedom Fighters

To the Freedom Fighters of SWAPO and ANC

Compatriots,
Ours is an unending struggle
Our ultimate goal of independence for our homeland
Is non-negotiable.

To this aim we dedicate
Our hearts and our minds
To this aim we dedicate
Our bodies and our lives
To this aim we dedicate
Our past, present and future
We dedicate everything.

For the struggle against apartheid inhumanity
We dedicate all for victory
For victory is certain
And we will win.

Compatriots
Ours is an unending struggle
We will move unrelentingly against the racists
We will march ever forward
We will turn back never
We will press ever onward
Firm in the faith that the final victory
Will be ours.

Compatriots,
Ours is an unending struggle
We know that the road will be long and tiring
We know that the mountains will be
Steep and perilous
We know that there will be pitfalls along the way
We know full well that our Freedom March
Will carry us across rivers of blood
Yet, we will press ever onward
Until we reach our destination
Firm in the faith that the final victory
Will be ours.

Compatriots,
Ours is an unending struggle
We will destroy the ulcers of colonial oppression
We will eliminate the festers of class exploitation
We will stamp out the cancers of white supremacy
From the face of the earth,
Now and forever.

Compatriots,
Ours is an unending struggle

The spear of Tshaka will hunt them down
The spear of Tshaka will put them to rout
The spear of Tshaka will drive them out
Of our homeland and bury their apartheid regime.

Compatriots,
Ours is an unending struggle
Only through armed power will we replace colonial domination
With a just and democratic social order:
That done, our children and our children's children
Will ever honor our memories,
Firm in the faith that the final victory
Will be ours.

Our battle cry:
One Namibia, one nation!
For a free Namibia—
One South Africa
One nation!
For a free South Africa!
Everything for the struggle against apartheid's inhumanity.

Everything for the struggle!
All for victory.
Victory is certain.
Compatriots,
We *will* win.

Margaret Burroughs

You Die in Pieces

To Nelson Mandela

Christ didn't want it either,
the cup of suffering—
sip it and sweat blood,
drink it and disappear
as a lover, a husband,
a father of daughters.
Your life is a concept.
You are a sacrament to your people.
Only pain is concrete—
twenty years in the black cell,
each false offer of freedom
a sheet of flesh torn
raw from the bone.
Economical lamb,
you can be slaughtered
again and again.
He only died once to save us,
but what a world
of ingenious darkness
you drew to save,
to be murdered
one cell at a time.

Sharon Cumberland
Brooklyn, New York

For Mandela

The chokers of "the Resistance" foolishly
watch their hands bleed and swell against the edge
on the struggle, your life, the people
entwined like a three strand rope
typing into a hangman's noose for
the death of apartheid

Karen Davis
Louisville, Kentucky
July 1988

I Honor You All

Let there be peace
Where you lie Chief
Brave Luthuli in the rich soil
Of the just

Let the evergreen spirit on
The spirit of revolution
To burn in the sinewy hearts
Of the sons and daughters
On the laboring soil

You are honored
You daughters of Africa
You whose wombs begot soldiers
Plodding the patriotic path
Of mother Africa

I honor you Duma Nokwe, Uncle J.B.
I honor you Mandela, Sisulu, Mlangeni
You whose minds shaped power
Plotting the maps of change
Sculptors of tomorrow

Goldberg, Bram Fischer, Kathrada
Are you not men
You whose sacrifice manned
The living soldiers

Peterson
Fallen body
Spirit of manhood
Rising ever to exist

Oh! Spirit of steel
Spirit that volunteers
Come spirit of Africa
Bring freedom
in our lifetime
Bring fighting freedom to our lives

Mpho Segomotso Dombo
South Africa

Hero of Heroes

Another dead body in the streets,
   "Imigqakhwana Yeetishala"
     -Bastards-
I cursed
as I struggled through the printed word.
They've turned this land
into a graveyard
where one day there won't be
marble enough
to honor all these youngsters
cut down so cruelly
in their prime;
   "Iqhawe Lama Qhawe"
     -Hero of Heroes-

who left no offspring
to swell the ranks
of the ancestral gods;
    "Iqhawe Lama Qhawe"
Monuments of Marble
in the South....

Vernon February
Amsterdam, the Netherlands
September 7, 1986

UDF Song

We came to Cape Town from the corners of this land
and we all met together, and we took up our stand
now there's nothing left to stop us under the sun
'til democracy's born and freedom's won.

Chorus:
Forward, forward with the UDF
the people united, will never be defeated
forward, forward, victory or death.

Well the people now are organized
to fight and resist the white state's lies
from coast to coast, and veldt to vlei
the boers will find there's hell to pay.

(*Chorus*)

Yes we're young and we're old, and we're black and we're white
and we know what's wrong, and we know what's right
we're workers, we're students, we're your community
and we won't stop 'til we've got freedom and democracy.

(Chorus)

There's those in the prisons, there's those who had to leave,
they're our fathers, sons and daughters, for them we grieve,
but Botha will grieve more if he doesn't soon declare
a constitutional conference with Mandela in the chair.

(Chorus)

Their bulldozers, their bullets, their police brutality,
don't frighten us, they help us to see
that fascism is evil, racism has no place
and apartheid's a crime against the whole human race.

(Chorus)

Well a struggle isn't easy, a struggle may be long
and taking power's more difficult than singing this song
but we'll take the pace, the hassles and the flak
cause we've started on the journey, and there's no turning back.

(Chorus)

We're the workers, we're the students, we're South Africa
we're the women, men and children,
in fact, to be blunt,
we're the national United Democratic Front.

Chorus:
Forward, forward with the UDF
the people united, will never be defeated
forward, forward, victory or death.

Patrick FitzGerald
South Africa
1983

42

Xhosa Chief
Nelson Mandela

Then the country was ours...the land, the forests, the rivers.

I
The Xhosa Chief says:
here is the boy
of the lambs,
this Transkei boy
who will hold Pretoria captive,
bound only by his daily breath,
waking in the African sun,
lying down in her slip-away arms.
That is how he will win,
this "kaffir,"
this black lion
who loves the veld.

II

What Pretoria must kill
is not simple.
Biko said it was a word:
Amandla!, so they killed Biko.
Children of Soweto said
it was language.
Before shooting Soweto boys,
Boer guards ordered:
Raise your fists, shout Amandla!
But only the boys fell.
Now they scrawl *Mandela*
on toilet stalls in Watts,
on prison walls in Manila, Rome, London
where patriots and pimps
mark their claims on destiny's
holding tanks, one
chalked, burned, carved
cry, amidst the foul, raging words.

Mandela is what they scratch.
It is all the pride some have left.

III

At the gate of Lincoln Park Zoo
on Chicago's North Side,
gardeners with quilters' eyes
sow patches of purple astor—aster—
twirls of marigold,
a circle of white geraniums
hover like moths, above
the mossy lawn. Trim.
Inside, in a new steel cage,
a languid lion places one
great paw after another,
silent, indifferent, as if
walking were a royal gesture.
He's dangerous, the white boys say.
The black girls rode two buses
from the South Side where
rivers of broken glass
run chippy over tin cans,
under abandoned cars,
glitter beneath a white neon moon.
Call that bad boy Mandela,
say the girls, he like a caged king, too.

IV

In 1964 Mandela spoke:
"It is an ideal for which
I am prepared to die."
As if the message were delayed,
the young ask: What did he say, Mamma?
Say that, Mandela, even in chains?
In the West, where faith is not easy,
the prophecy repeats over and over,
this Transkei boy
they could not kill him.

Golden

44

Freedom

The stone
wrapped clumsily
in your tiny fist,
driven through the air
with language
yet alien to your sweet tongue:
the only cry
that splits your plucked lips
the primal shout of hope,
kneaded into the missile
and nurtured
until its release from
the fluid arc of your arm.

Freedom
you remember in your stoop
is always one stone away.

Rajen Govender
South Africa

To Nelson Mandela

The tree has not borne fruit
But the branches are sprouting
Can you not see!
Can you not hear!

You cannot see
How can you?
Behind those high walls
The high fences
The watchful guards
The malignant system

You can hear
How can you not
Those thunderous voices
Screaming in pain and enthusiastic
anger
The thunder

It is not a dream
Voices heard are angry
With your spirit
Entangled with theirs
In immortal combat

The tree has not borne fruit
But the branches are sprouting
To bear fruit
Where you are chained

Nelson Mandela
 Nelson Mandela
  Nelson Mandela
   Nelson Mandela
    Nelson Mandela
     Nelson Mandela
      Nelson Mandela
       Nelson Mandela

Munyonzwe Hamalengwa
Downsview, Ontario, Canada
February 22, 1984

Birthday Haiku Blessing

In tribute to Nelson Mandela and the struggle for freedom, justice and peace in South Africa

The sunrise will melt
captivity's ice blanket
and end its frostbite.

Nkosi Sikelela

Correctus Historum

We browned and blackened bodies resound
ancient chimes in bones fleshed with
labor sore arms, tire and flounder.
Beg time to wait for breath to catch up
for hearts to slow.

We hands and legs to whom is given
a curse of work and a bucket of water
to wash, to drench, to drink and
be renewed to work again and again;
to fulfill the prophecy—beg to see
the god and decree of words and deeds
who contracted an eternal work force.

We wish to know why mercy does not stay
slavers' chains, nor lands from colonial might.
We pray for a promise of divine intervention
fearing as we bend, stand, kneel, that this
is the one (or ones) who hears . . . (hear!)

47

We song and voice in a barren land
or dance and drum hidden deep in bush
cry our long sufferings to the wind.
Our gods have become phantoms. We doubt
if they ever existed. It has been so long
since we have seen them. We thus roam
in an unfriendly world looking for a
kindness which is strong enough to change
the course of our lives. We run from
god to gods, house to field; a voice,
a hand—foot upon ground, truly beggars.
Our icons are locked up and guarded from us.
We are born and die never seeing them.
Our parents say it was not always so
but we, their agnostics, beg the question;
"If they did exist, where are they now?"

We have questions but no answers.
Our parents have not enough faith
to convince us that our hands can
be used for other than toiling for others.
We who have given so much received so little.
Our patience is tried again and again.
Our resolve falters. Steps fall further
and further behind our leaders.
We question our own strength.
And bow again and again before
the weight of gold buried deep
beneath brass.

And now, in spite of our own cowardice,
our chance comes to reinstate icons of old
invoke gods buried beneath pagan churches
where mercy was shut out. And we rise.
We rise to greet the joy of a sun filled day.

We run to embrace browned and blackened arms
of our families, millions strong. We sing
a mighty war song. We dance in communion!
We gather across the land,
by the river,
in the bush,
behind high rise city dwellings.
We march! We march!

We will once again sing
our old songs of joy.
Call our gods to come to us
in a language we understand.
And we who have given to others
so much give to ourselves
our strength. Our best!
And beg our gods
to give us more to give
to this world we make
with our own hands.

(Testament to Winnie Mandela)

Rashidah Ismaili
New York, New York

Pedigree, with Weight

(Matouba, Basse Terre, 1802)

this island now
beautiful as suicide.

49

and so then
the hair burn down to meet the ankle bone.

basse terre but this island low!
    even so
there is dryness in all:
this water and craft
lithe schooners, bilanders
the way past the whorehouses in port
soft sockets in the groin
   vile mouth vile insuck and vileness of feeling
(food and drink for a long voyage)

this island and a black business
to make a point white:
"but the land low; there was the yellow fever
the disorder of salted meat
dry biscuit and cask
to sweeten an old wrong"

and so then
the hair burn down to meet a man's ankle bone
and the sun ramble over,
totally other, a turmoil of skeletons
and sourness to no real purpose

"gun powder makes for transient names.
and after all this what is Matouba?
stillness and clarity of detail,
a torn hand, a torn jaw
bone cracked on a stone ledge,
will not help will not help"

this island basse terre bent
low and the thing continue
cape to caribbean sea
and the thing reach so under a man
to squeeze the heart out of all jubilation

and what if a man can move still
pedigreed with weight; what if a man get up
and move so
like god's self footloose in egypt,
    at war and still
with firstborn fly and plague...

Lemuel Johnson
Ann Arbor, Michigan

Ah! Rholihlahla!!

Mzi wakowethu, ukwenjenje, asikuba sihlabela iGwatyu,* koko sithe
namhlanje makhe siyithuke le nkwenkwe yakwa Ngubengcuka.

Lent' umntu asinto ukuvunywa ligama layo,
Athi khon' ukuba ngowegazi
Suka into le igqithise.

Waathi ubulixhiba
Suk' uJongintaba wakutyumba
Waza kubek' eziko koMkhulu
Kwa No-Inglani, inkosikazi,
Imaz' ebele lide, intombi ka Krune.
KoMkhulu aph'izithethe ezi zomzi
Neenkcukacha zokukhonz' isizwe
Zifundwa khona.
Wathi mhla wakusoka wakubulisa
Ngelika "Rholihlahla"
Nokwesazi nje ukub' ihlal' eli

*iGwatyu—yingoma yomknosi, ekuphunywa ngayo ukuya kuhlangabeza
utshaba. Eka Cetywayo ngu "Malombo." aphuma ngay' amaBandl' akhe
ngemini yase Sandlwana.

51

Yint' ezele ngameva
Kanye nawobobo, nawomqaqoba.

Ulishiy' elakowenu uselula; waya kwel' eGoli;
eGoli, aph' umntu lo angazelwe nto;
Ath' ebezaz' engumntu; kanti namhla woba ngu Kafile.
eGoli, aph' isabhokwe seBhulu
Sidada komnyama nowegazi.
Wothuka, wathimla, wathimba, Nkonyane yoHlanga;
Kube nje wena zange wayibona;
Wondliwa, wakhuliswa ngeyokuba
Umntu lo unesidima nesithozelo
Kungoko afanelwe yimbeko.

Livakel' izwi lakho phakathi kwama khaba
Likhalima, likhuza lempathw' inje.
Asandule sithembe, sisithi ligazi lishushu,
Ngamabhongo namatshamb' obutsha,
Lusana lubhibhidl' amazinyo.
Engu Hal' obhuzubhuzu nje
Bukroti abuchole phi?
Kanti silibala eyona ndoqo
Kumntu lo yena olandel' ikhazi
Kubuzalwa ngu Nosekeni, um-Mpemvukazi
AmaMpemvu, iiNjoli kaloku
Kuma zikw' enkundla zakwa Phalo

Kuse Goli aph' udibene
NomQwathikazi, intombi ka Mase;
Nobabini niselula; ulityendyana lomfana.
Yakwakha, yakululeka, yakuqinis' ufokotho;
Yakukhuthaza, yakufutha de wafutheka
Ube nje namhla nakwezomthetho waseSilungwini
UyiNcutshe, kwezesizwe ugqwesile,
Yathi yakukhov'ukucola de wacoleka:
'Naanko ke, Mzi we Afrika, ngowenu
Nanithe kaloku ngu Rholihlahla,
Ndosala ndigcin' ikhaya mna

52

Ndinondlela uThembisile, no Makgatho, noMakaziwe'.
Uthini na ke umzi ukungabuleli, Mqwathikazi?

Yath' isitsho, yab' ikuyaleza kweyamaMpondo
Ku Nomzamo, iqhajikasi elingeva ntambo
Lentombi zakwa Ngutyana,
Elathi lifika, labe selisithi:
'Ungaxhali, Madiba, sendikho,
Nawomqaqoba mna ndowabangula,
Ndinyathel' aph' unyathela khona
Ndiyi ntonga' kwesekhosi.
Lirhole eli hlahla, Duna lakwa Hala,
Linameva linjalo, lirhole;
Umzi wakowenu ubanjwe ngawobobo,
Uminxwe awukwazi nokuphefumla.
Ubangafun' ukubek' unyawo
Kuthiwe: "Nyawuka! Nyawuka!"
Ubangazam' ukunaba
Ibe ngu: "Finyela! Finyela! Finyela!"

Kungoko uziphose wonke kweli dabi,
Idabi lenkululeko yomzo wakowenu.
Lavakala kalokw' igalelo lakho;
Macalan' onke watsh'umthinjana nomlisela
Wathi: 'Tshotsholoza Mandela
Beth' iinduku mfana'
Batsho koqhel' ukuzibetha
Kulomathaf' ase Qweqwe nase Mqhekezweni;
Batsho kokwaz' ukucel umNgeni
Koma Qunu nakoma Qokolweni.
Bathi: 'Tshotsholoza Mandela
Beth' iinduku mfana
Uyakuva ngathi
Xa sekulungile.

Uzibethile mfana ka Henry, ngalo min' emkhumbini;
Wazibek' aph' iinyaniso zadandalaza;
Kwathi qwenge, kwasa kwathi gede,
Kwabona nemfama, kweva nesithulu;

53

Mhl' amaDlagusa ayekutyhola
Ngele Mvukelo-mbuso.
Watsho Madiba ungenadyudyu, ungenavalo.

'Ndisivil' isimbonono sesikhalo somzi endinguwo
Umzi oncwina phantsi kwedyokhwe yengcinezelo
Ohlafuna isonka sembandezelo, usela amanzi engqalekiso;
Umzi endinguwo, osikhalo singasiwe-so
Ngumbuso welilizwe, esiphantsi kwawo.

Eso sikhalo satsho kwasik' emazantsi;
Ndikhumbul' ukub' ookhokho, kanene,
Bafa belilwela, bezam' ukulihlangula;
Laahluthwa kubo ngamaqhinga nekrele;
Namhla bazibeka, yayingekuba boyisiwe,
Koko yayikurhola, ukuz' idibane ngomso,
Benethemba lokuba lobuyiswa kwa ngekrele
Sithi sizukulwana sabo.
Kungoko ndithe: "iNguqu, Mzi wakowethu!
Lifikil' ixesha lokub' idibane;
Lilelethu nje, lobuyiswa kwasithi.
Ma-Hala! Akukho nkunzi yakha yoyiswa
Kobakowayo!!
Mhlekazi, ukuba ezi nyaniso yo-Mvukelo-mbuso
Makube kunjalo ke, Ndixolele ukufa"

Awu! Hay' ezalo mini ma Afrik' amahle!
Mhla watheth' umfana ka Henry kwalum' ekhosi;
Ndithi, yakhula le kwekwe, yakhula sijongile;
Yakhula, yagabadela,
Yadlul' ezongcungela zomthetho zazikulo nkundla'
Lay' eligama: "Mhlekazi, ukuba le nyaniso
Yi-Mvukelo-mbuso, makube kunjalo ke. Ndixolele ukufa"
Litsho nzulu kwabanesazela, nabantliziyo zinyulu.

Adideka kalokw' amaDlagusha aziphunguzulu
Anevuso, axak' ukuba angenza yiphi na.
Anga angakugwebela intambo,
Hayi abuy' umva, kub' enje inyaniso

Ayifi namntu wayo, ayifi kuxhonywa.
Lay' ilizwi lakho litsho ngomtyangampo
Ozalis' onk' amagumb' omhlaba.
Kungoko akuthe nka ngolayifu esiQithini
Ngelawo ekungcwaba uhleli
Elibal' eyokuba inyaniso yona ayina ngcwaba.

Loo mazwi akho alo mini emkhumbini
Ahlal' ehlel'ezingqondweni zomzi wakuni;
Namhla aphindwa zimveku zayizolo
Ezingazanga zakwalama ngeliso lenyama
Koko zikuv' ezimbalini zeli dabi lenkululeko.
Kutsh' uluntu namhlanje kumbombo zone zomhlaba
"Mkhululen' uMadiba kunye nezozigidi zikweso siQithi"
Livakala kwezi ntlambo: Bakhululeni!
Lisatyelwa yilaa nkalo: Bakhu-lu-le-ni!!
Lihlokoma kula mawa: Ba-khu-lu-le-ni!!'.
Sisankxwe, inkxuba-xaka
Etshw' amaDlagush' ema nemata, angamayilo.

"Makaginye laa mazwi omhla wesigwebo,
Somkhulula, icekwa likuye"
Watsh' udyakalash' omaqhinga.
"Linani kakade", yatsh' impendulo,
"Sikun' inj' isitshixo
Sokuvula ezi ngcango.
Ndawaginya?
Ndingawaginya njani ngomzi wakowethu
Osabotshwe inyawo nezandla,
Olizwi selatsha lathi khothe
Kukhala kungekho usabelayo?
Wakh' umntu lo wananisa na
Ngobuntu obu bakhe?
Singathetha njani nani, thina sisenkampini?
Vulan' iingcango nathi singene
Kwiinkundla zelizwe loobawo,
Siqingqi' imithetho yentlalo yezwe lethu,
Sizathuze nathi, sifuzis' okwamandulo."

Madiba, ngath' umzi wakuni phandl' apha, wanele;
Ngath' uthand' ukuthi: "Yidibe, Madiba
Kufayayo, ukufa kunye kunkongolo;
Liphelil' iphaphu, nentaka, nevuso;
Sesimi ngawe uze kuyifunza.
Tshotsholoza, Mandela,
Shay' induku, mfana,
Yizwa ngathi, sekulungile
Singawucel' umNgeni.

Ungamshiy' uXhamela, igwangqa lika Sisulu,
Nguye kaloku owobamb' ihlelo
Mhla sayifunza.
Engu Mqwathi nje akalwaz' udum' ekhosi.
Uthath' iZiz' elo lakwa Jama,
uGovan ka Mbek' eMpukane,
Abe ludondolo
Esova ngalo esi ziba mhla sawela;
Ikwa nguye kaloku owosintsokothela
Eze ntlalo nokumiwa kwelizwe elitsha,
Ilizwe lakwa Nkululeko.

Uqul' ulugangathe ngoka Mhlaba noka Mlangeni,
Eyokurhola ingoka Motswaledi; eyokungena ingoka
     Kathrada;
Uz' uphahlwe yilo nginginya yama Afrika
Bawavalele kweso siQithi;
Sokwazi ngawo thina, mhla wavela
Sikuhlangabeza, siyimbumba yamanyama;
Sizekuthi kuba Bandezeli bethu:
Singabomgquba, Singaboluthuthu,
VULANI, SINGENE!"

Nogqaza we Jojo
Cape Town, South Africa

Ah! Rholihlahla!!

Fellow Africans, we are not by this Song starting a war cry.*
But we felt you had to hear a thing or two about this son of the
House of Ngubengcuka.

A man, they say, usually lives up to his name,
And this is only too true when such is of royal birth.

Though you were of a minor house, the iXhiba
Jongintaba picked you
Brought you to the Royal Home
To the house of No-Inglani, his wife
The woman with the long breast, daughter of Krune,
To the Royal Home, fount of the culture
And custom of a people
The Royal Home where the art of service
To the nations is learnt.
And when he initiated you into manhood
He saluted you with the name "Rholihlahla"
Full knowing that such a bough sometimes
Bristles with thorns
Even those of the thistle and the thornbush.

A mere youth, you left home for eGoli
eGoli where man has no worth
eGoli where he who prided himself
Of his humanhood now becomes just a Kaffir
eGoli where the sjambok of the whiteman
Lashes indiscriminately the commoner
And him of royal birth.
Amazed, shocked, you protested
Young calf of the royal herd
For such you had never known before
You were nurtured and taught
That Man was a noble being
Full of dignity, humanity and grace
And as such worthy of respect.

Rholihlahla—He who pulls along the severed bough (i.e. does not shirk his duty).

Soon your voice was heard among the youth
Condemning and protesting such treatment
At first, we were not impressed
Dismissing it as the gallantry of an angry young man
His blood hot with the fervour of youth,
A baby teething, blowing to cool his gums
"He is of the House of Hala," we said
"The Hala, cowards among the nations
Where then would he get such courage?"
We were missing the truth, however,
That a man will follow his father's cattle
Take something from his mother's people;
For, is he not the son of Nosekeni of the ama-Mpemvu
The ama-Mpemvu, Masters of Ceremony
In the courtyards of the House of Phalo?

It was at eGoli, you met the woman
Of the ama-Qwathi, daughter of Mase.
You were both young; you a youthful dandy.
She groomed and molded you;
Nurtured and cultivated you
As a mother her child;
She inspired and encouraged you,
So, today you are expert in the White Man's law
And in the affairs of the nation, among the best.
And when her task was done
She turned you over to the nation, saying:
"There he is, my people. He is yours!
You called him 'Rholihlahla'
I will remain behind in the house
Rearing for you his offspring
Thembisile, Makgatho and Makaziwe."
How then, can the nation not give thanks
To you daughter of the ama-Qwathi?

So saying she entrusted you to the Mpondo woman
Nomzamo, the high-spirited, unbridled
Bold daughter of the House of Ngutyana
Who, on arrival said: "Fear not Madiba;
I am here already;
I'll pull out of your feet even the hardest of thorns.
Treading in your footsteps

I'll be your eyes, your ears, your defender;
Pull along this bough, son of the House of Hala
Even though bristling with thorns, bring it along
Your people are as a lamb caught in the thistle bush
They cannot breathe;
They know not where to turn.
When they try to move, it is: 'Go back! Go Back!'
When they try to settle down, it is: 'Not here!
Not here!! Not here!!!' "

Then it was you threw yourself
into the struggle
The struggle for the liberation of your people.
Soon your presence was noted;
From all sides, young men and women
Sang: "Slink in the shadows, Mandela
Hitting hard with your stick."
Said this to one who wielded that stick well
In the plains of Qweqwe and Mqhekezweni
To an adept at surprising and challenging
The youth of Qunu and Qokolweni.
"Slink in the shadows, Mandela,
Hit hard with your stick.
You will hear from us when we are ready."

You wielded that stick well, son of Henry
On that day in the law court;
Brought out all the facts, for all to see.
Everything was clear, as clear as day.
Even the blind could see, and the deaf hear.
This was the day the regime waas accusing
You of high treason.
Madiba, you spoke without fear or favor
"I have heard the wailing of my people,
My people groaning under the yoke of oppression,
A people chewing the bread of despair,
And drinking the waters of damnation.
My people whose cry is not heeded
By the government under which we serve.

"That cry tore the very guts of my being.
I remembered that our forefathers

Died, fighting to save this land;
It was taken from them through guile
And at the barrel of the gun;
Even, when they laid down their arms
It was not to accept defeat,
But to recoup after a battle lost
With the knowledge that through war
And blood, it would be regained
By us, the future generation.
So it was, I said to my comrades
A change of course, my countrymen
The time has come to regain our land
We, and we alone can do it
I swear by the House of Hala
No bull has ever been driven
Out of its own cattle-fold
Your Worship, if this truth be treason.
So be it. I am prepared to die."

Awu: What a day noble sons
And daughters of Afrika!!
The day when this boy of Henry spoke.
Spoke, and our hair stood on end!!
The boy grew, grew in stature
Before our very eyes!
He stood tall; towered over all those Giants of Law
In that courtroom
And these words: "Your worship, if this truth be
treason
So be it. I am prepared to die."
Struck home in the minds of those with a conscience
And the pure of heart.

He damned and confounded his accusers.
The regime was at a loss;
They did not know what to do.
At first, they considered sentencing him to death;
Pondered and retreated,
Remembering that the truth does not die
With the one who spoke it.
The truth cannot be hanged.
And his final words in that law court

Had filled the four corners of the world.
Then, they sentenced him to life in prison
Hoping thereby to bury him alive
Forgetting that the truth defies even the grave.

Your words in that law court that day
Remained forever in the minds of your people
Today they are repeated by children of yesterday;
Children who never saw or knew you,
But know of you as one of the heroes
In the struggle for freedom.
People, today, throughout the world are clamoring
"Release Mandela and all those others
You've confined on Robben Island."
Even these valleys are calling: "Release Mandela"
The hilltops answer the call: "Release Mandela"
The very mountains echo it: "Release Mandela"
It is ceaseless clamour
That has puzzled the regime to no end.

"Let him renounce violence
We will release him," said the wily jackal
"The ball is in your court," was your reply.
"For it is you who holds the keys to open
These doors.
Renounce violence?
How can I when my people
Are still bound hand and foot,
Their voices hoarse with crying
With no one heeding that cry?
What man has ever sold his birthright
For a mess of pottage?
How can my people begin to talk with you
When they are held in bondage?
Open the doors so that we, too, may come in,
Where, we, too, will formulate the laws
To govern our land. . .
Give our best for the good of our land
Just as our forefathers were wont to do.

Madiba, your people out here have had enough!
They seem to want to say: "Give the word, Madiba

Make the call! Only those who dare ever win
Death is harsh; death is cruel.
No doubts still linger; all fear is gone
We are waiting on you to give the word.
Move stealthily, Mandela; slink in the shadows
Hitting hard with your stick,
Hear us now; we are ready
To take on the enemy!"

Don't leave Xhamele behind, the light-skinned
Son of Sisulu;
It is he who will command the flank
On the day of battle.
He is Qwathi, the Qwathi who bear
No wounds on the backs of their heads.
Bring along that Zizi of the house of Jama
Govan Mbeki of Mpukane is his name
He will be the long staff with which
We test the waters of the deep pools
On the day we cross over.
It is he also who will teach and guide us
In the ways of governing and living
In the new land,
The land of freedom, equality and humanity

The son of Mhlaba and the son of Mlangeni
Will be your defending stick
With which you ward off the enemy.
With the son of Motswaledi as your long stick
You will feel out and draw the enemy;
For close combat, pull out your short stick
The son of Kathrada.
Come to us surrounded by those hundreds,
Of our people they've confined on that Island
It is by their company, we will recognize you
When, united, we come out to meet
And welcome you
All coming to tell our oppressors
"We are of the kraal manure;
We are of this soil,
This is our LAND!
OPEN THE DOOR!!"

Nogqaza we Jojo
Cape Town, South Africa

Every Patriot a Combatant

Though I do not howl like the Wolf
I could go down slow
Or jump back bad and light fires
To burn down granite
Or toi-toi from the future
With the elegance of people's power

Yes Mbeki I know a woman out in Mexico
Whose Zapata heart and eye are worldwide
And her eye heaves with a force
More powerful than the floods

There walks Chris Hani
Across the River Mockba
On his way to South Africa
With the future
Hammered to steel in his eye
Shaping every patriot into a combatant

La Guma tell us about the logic of history
About the threefold cord
You weave our spirit into
Here in this stone country
At the fog of the seasons' end
Where infants with clenched fists
Kick terror in her vampire teeth

MAYIHLOME!

Keorapetse Kgositsile
Lusaka, Zambia

December Sixteen

Comrades
I was not there
On December 16, 1961
And you probably were not there either

We neither heard Mandela's trumpet
Stirring and mustering to national duty
Millions of poised waiting lions
Nor were we in Tambo's mind
As he carried us around the globe
Dissecting for the world to see
Our land and fields overflowing
With rivers and rivers
Of our own precious blood
Perhaps, we didn't even feel
The pounding hammering thrill
Inside Sisulu's heart
As he helped forge
and wield UMKHONTO WE SISWE
But comrades
though we were not there
At those meandering underground journeys
Voyages into daylight of victory
No comrades
Absent, we were very much there
For we recall now and relive today
The supreme challenge
Of the true leader of our people
Chief Albert Mvumbi Luthuli
When that magnificent giant of a lion roared
And the thunder and tremor of his words
Still echo in our consciences, our consciousness
This day

"I am an African
And if the enemy comes into my home
To attack both myself and my family
Then I as an African
Must take up my spear and fight"

Yes Comrades
Absent we were there
Because we all now agree
That this pain
Will not repair
Before the sharpening of all our spears
Deep inside racist and fascist bones
To hunt and haunt the enemy
Out of our home, our social equal home.

Lindiwe Mabuza
South Africa

Mandela and All Comrades in Prison

You are just number 466/64 to them
sweeping dusty paths
tilling and raking the soil of that island.

But you are the strength,
the determination
that flows through the veins of your children
fighting for you
you and all those numbers.

Yes, with your spade firmly in your hand
till and rake the soil Mandela
like your brothers, sisters, sons and daughters
who toil and sweat for Africa:

She is ours
we too shall know no rest
till she comes back to us.

Ilva Mackay
South Africa

This Country is Turmoil

this river
    this country in turmoil
    may the first grade garden
    fruit in the splendor of commitment

these are mighty
footsteps the way
pointing the way back back there
where mothers kiss the burning walls
of tears

they cannot be consoled
nor made to break with what is
for their pain is loud with meaning
not the hyperbole of prayers

now I must break with this language
I must simply say
    I love my country my mother
    my kisses bring death and life
    I'll say to the worker...arise
    bring the harvest into the fold
    and distate the menu the recipes
    of your life
is this simple now no no
I have failed to tell my mother who she is
now what we are to each other
and to the world

I have failed to cry like a committed son
I have hiccupped when the communion
of spears was served
and at the grave-side site I have murdered
my ancestors with cowardice
I need blood river
and the battle dust and the sighing gasps
must cleanse my lungs
shall I come out a new man at dawn
when the elephants bathe in the valley
of blood
shall I talk to the lost spears
whose language is hot vengeance
shall I talk to the lost spears
this lost garden this mother
I'll kiss the drought away
and this revolution this mother blood
shall fruit the inevitable

I have lost my tongue in slavery
I must find it in the new flag
and start to learn from scratch to say
black
green
and
gold

where is love in the smiles
of starving children and
breaking muscles
and unpaid sweat
what do we grasp from laughter
of the homeless
and the hopes of mothers
at the grave-side

at the grave-site

there'll be blows at this grave-side
we'll stand on the wombs of our mothers
and labor
I hear the wind of the song
and the chant of triumph
and the philosophy of fruit
breaking the separating lines of the world
bringing together the sweat and the elbows
of productive mankind

this is the forge of the new republic
black green and gold
of a new world
a society of a heart married
to a history of eyes

this world this land this mother
has seen this country

    this river in turmoil
    may the first grade garden
    fruit in the splendor of our commitment.

Victor Matlou
South Africa

A Song for Mandela

Inside of me
    In this blackened casket
    wounds lie sealed like bodies in vault;
    shouts of anger crackle like flames
    in the fireplace of injustice

Beneath me
  impatient tremors burst out
  to break the dry olive branch of peace
  sold at the marketplace of deception
Around me
  the precious womb that bled me to life;
  flesh that clothed my soul
  and gave it wings...
      Yet even a mother's love
      Is fragile to torment and to terror
Beside me
  heavy footfalls of running men
  cries of thwarted souls rush like restless rain
  from the skies of despair
Near me
  I hear the staunch march of anxious feet
  carrying the sounds of defiance
      Not alone, God not alone
      Will we rise up to repossess ourland
      Truth is witness to our wrath
      and our commitment
      Evil has had its day...
Beside me,
  Around and beneath me;
  Inside this burning self
  Where impatient drums
  Beat a martial song
  I hear Mandela singing:
      Unzima lomtwalo
      Ufuna amadoda...

Don Mattera
Johannesburg, South Africa

(From *Azanian Love Song*,
Skotaville Publishers,
Johannesburg, South Africa)

69

A Happy Birthday to a Hero—
Dr. Nelson Rolihlahla Mandela

(On his 70th anniversary)

Three scores and a decade of survival
for the Father of our Revolution,
who rides on the red wings of our hopes,
the galloping Steed of black aspiration,
frisky for a fight for freedom.

To seek the crown
To reclaim the throne of victory
for the liberated land of sunlit skies and crimson clouds,
for the rich gold bullion reefs in our Eldorado—
the fabulous Eureka lined with numerous precious minerals
the dazzling Big Holes aglitter with diamonds of Kimberley—
the verdant meadows and pastures with grazing cattle and wild game,
the fertile wheatlands and cornfields and golden orchards,
to feed the multitudes of all the thirty million citizens.

Scion of timeless resistance to blood-thirsty conquerors,
intruders bearing blazing the flag of racism;
Paragon of our perseverance and Pillar of justice,
Fearless Fighter of numerous battles
through Treason Trials and Rivonia tribulations
with comrades united
in love and loyalty for the fatherland and Mother Africa;
To face incarceration with unwavering bravery
multiplied into a quarter century of unflagging fortitude and fearlessness,
your spirit, your will, your power unbroken,
your influence
to young and old rising daily to dizzying heights
despite the frightened Foe cracking the whip
to keep the proletariat in a perpetual state of oppression
while the National's Treasure-Trove is plundered.

Proud Bearer and Warrior of the Spear of the Nation—
Umkhonto we Sizwe—
the blood-lipped weapon of our liberation
from the dark dungeons of apartheid
and appalling cells of torture and torment,
where ruthless jailers thought
the sun would set on you
and cast its evil shadow of despair
and swallow you into the belly of oblivion.

Like a Colossus indomitable
you have remained a symbol of our strength,
a badge of our invincibility
on the international horizon as well as at home,
where all freedom loving patriots await
you with garlands of triumph and jubilation
to celebrate with many martyrs and freedom fighters
Liberation Day
on which you will declare the Peoples' Republic of Amandlavia.

Mbuyiseni Oswald Mtshali
Brighton
Boston, Massachusetts

When the Ghost of Benjamin Moloise Appears*

It will be a great day
It will be a terrible day
    when the ghost of Benjamin Moloise appears...

*Benjamin Moloise, activist-poet executed by the apartheid regime for high
treason in 1982; high treason being his aid in the struggle against apartheid.

The earth will be quaking
The clouds will be screeching
   when the ghost of Benjamin Moloise appears...

Hundreds and thousands of children
will be dancing in the streets
   when the ghost of Benjamin Moloise appears...

The catacombs of the robben islands will open
The rivers will flood the land with freedom
   when the ghost of Benjamin Moloise appears...

The mandelas of the land will be reunited
The supremacy of the reactionary will rip apart at the seams
The sun will begin a long eeeeerie laugh
   when the ghost of Benjamin Moloise appears...

And he will rise from the bleeding soil
a thousand times larger than life
The graves at dimbaza will split open at his beckoning
All the children slaughtered by these devils
will also rise a thousand times larger than life
They will still be wet and warm
where they were mortally wounded
They will march on the last throes of this monster
chanting a bloodcurdling chant
   "for what crime was I killed?!
   for what crime was I KILLED?!!!"
    when the ghost of Benjamin Moloise appears

Diehard boars will incinerate themselves in their nuclear arsenals tusk-in-earth
   when the ghost of Benjamin Moloise appears...

The most sick of these diehards
hellbent on going down fighting to the last man
will
go
down
   when the ghost of Benjamin Moloise appears...

72

But it will be his voice
back from the dead
terrible and determined
that will part day and night at high noon!
It will be the clamoring
reverberating
harmonic shrill of his voice
that will freeze this moment for immortality!
It will be his voice
haunting
bonechilling
reaching from where the rope ripped his throat
and snapped his neck in two
that will crack this monster's skull
melt its brains
rupture its eardrums
bust its bowels
choke and blowout its heart!!!
It will be his voice
the nerveshredding voice of Benjamin Moloise
that will deal
the ultimate
      death
        to
          apartheid...

Zayid Muhammad
New York, New York
April30, 1987

73

Nomzamo[1]

(For all the strong women of South Africa)

Nomzamo, your look is filled with pain and sorrow
And your tears mean more than broken dreams
Your daughters sit beside you as you look into the distance
And your husband may never come back home
Where do you get the strength to carry on?

Uwafumana phi na amandla angaka okuqhubeka?[2]

Nomzamo, the look in your eyes cannot be borne
Pain too great for me to understand
is this wonder woman's constant companion
You carry on with amazing grace
Where do you get the strength to carry on?

Uwafumana phi na amandl' okuqhubeka?

Nomzamo, the thunder from the storm
is a lullaby to your ears
used to the cacophony of bullets bursting all around you
Where does your strength come from
When you've been struggling for so long?

Uwafumana phi na amandl' okuqhubeka?

Nomzamo, your look is filled with pain and sorrow
And your tears mean more than broken dreams
Your daughters sit beside you as you look into the distance
And your husband my never come home
Where do you get the strength to carry on?

---

[1] Nomzamo, Winnie Mandela's Xhosa name, is derived from the noun "ukuzama"; the name connotes perseverance and relentless struggle.
[2] Where do you get the strength to carry on?

Uwafumana phi na amandla angaka?

Mbulelo Mzamane
Athens, Georgia

For Nelson Mandela

Nelson, in this your 70th year
grace and pardon to your oppressors.
Your life spent in chains
now crowns the rock of justice,
of judgement.
Your life the pride and dignity of
people who bow in homage;
Live on to see
Alsatians at children's throats,
die of their own poison
like the caged serpent
in Pretoria's State House.

Mandela: from deepest Olduvai
where men first blinked
at the sun's power
first contemplated the stars in canopy
your volcanic strength pours out against
tyranny.

The tower of Apartheid
Crumbles at the edges
It quakes from within
and spews out torrents
of diabolical gall, before demise.
The time is not yet
but written clear
though the powerful stand vigil.

The inspiration of truth comes,
not as a valiant rider
or the demented hurricane,
not as the all-destructive missile,
but in the stealth of might
on sweet gossamer wings.

Few are blessed
to receive and hearken
you are of that number.

Lenrie Peters

Who Am I?

I am the souls
That emerge from the stench
and gutter of oppression.

I am the ghost
of that man the fascist maimed
    in Sharpeville
of that child Vorster killed in
Langa-Gugulethu-Soweto...

I am the spirit
of Makana returning from
    Robben Island prison
to remind the enemy
that the struggle continues.

I am the poison-that-can-heal
that is the meal that P.W.
    Botha
will have for his last supper.
I am a revolution sure of its
victory.

Flaxman Qoopane
South Africa

Tribute to Nelson Mandela

along this road of war
hands have hewed the rocks
muscles have spoken tales
and streets have been built
where casspirs run and ruin
but still those very roads
have opened paths to freedomways
your hands are there too
stumping pulp Robben Island stone

you and we have signed
a scroll on white sheet
Graffitti on tanned walls
on marula bark trees
a pact with freedom
an incision of black green
and gold strands
on the mountain tops
of Isandlwana's hillocks

you have bitten the road
with muscles and heart and soul
you have pounded this cheeky path
and where you stand footsteps
remain
yes they remain forcibly
along this road of war
footsteps race and gallop with potency
MANDELA HAPPY BIRTHDAY
for those 70 heartbeats
we still wait for your homecoming.

Rebecca
South Africa
July 1988

77

Mandela

Now the moon has glazed over kraals
And stars flash their eyes for the septuagenarian:
It is the cockcrow of unrelieved celebration.

Dreams have long been nurtured, hopes tended:
It is time to celebrate the immanent possibility.
Though thorns have lurked to impede youthful impatience
And wives have waited in the solemnity of their huts
And the tender gardeners have raked the ground
For the longed-for coming, there is still for you
The unrelieved waiting.

Let them speak in tongues of unsculptured stone.
They have become edifices of wrong, monuments
Of a sacred myopia. They have dragged their
Crocodile-backs with the holiness of vultures.
They hover over a lush terrain
With the conscience of a Dark Age.

What other sacrifices do they call and ask for?
Do they command?
And should there be any more speech,
If speech is only the syllable of Order?
Should there be, when all around is
The chaos of conscience?

Let the elders plead in sorry-tongues of forgiveness.
And let the youth trail on the path of a bulldozer-calling.
And let myth be created and myth be disseminated
About the septuagenarian who pays the dues of white-hairs
For the permanent love of his people.

We need the perpetual myth,
The distilled myth of him, pure as African gold.

For now that the moon has glazed over kraals,
And the memory of Tshaka parades the falling white-dawn,
It is time for unrelieved celebration.

Tijan M. Sallah
Greensboro, North Carolina

Our Army

In the middle of the night
They woke us
To move us
As the enemy was expected.

Outside in the darkness
I stumbled,
Almost fell.

A comrade steadied me
and took
The sleeping baby
From my arms
And handed me his AK.

M. Schoon
South Africa

Can I Get a Witness Here

How shall I tell them at home
That I met you at Grenoble
Beneath the slopes of the snow-capped Alps
Father Nelson Mandela

79

How can I make anyone believe
That the streets were full of you
In Grenoble outside the gates of Pollsmoor Prison
Father Nelson Mandela

Who can help tell everyone how your face
Loomed large in a city older than your country
Dressed warmly in a polo-neck jersey
Father Nelson Mandela

You stood far from the Koeberg nuclear station
Yet so very near the French nuclear power monster
Enclosed within the majestic towering Alps
Father Nelson Mandela

Up there on the slopes of the Alps
A thousand feet up the tumbling green slopes
I stood looking at the city below
Pondering the meaning of a place
Unwashed for centuries
A Roman abode in times past
At peace with itself
No fusses of centenary celebrations
Whose yield demeans the human heart
With such guilt as Operation Hunger
Amidst the glitter of gold and diamonds
I was standing where I could pluck off clouds
The air was a fresh green smell
Clean
Neat
Pure
All around there was the cherry-tree in bloom
With lily-white flowers
All around there was the apple-tree in bloom
With dazzling pink flowers
All around there was a mass of pine-trees
Stubbornly green all seasons
As defiant as the massive rocks

And the high peaks of the Alps
Wearing white caps all seasons
And then all at once I felt a moving spirit
My heart's pounding beat
In unison with the enthralling sights about me
The ring of rugged timeless mountains
The rolling green sides of these high sentinels
And oh! I saw the serene face of
Father Nelson Mandela
As if indifferent to the words scrolled
Over and below his sublime face
In a bleeding red color
    LIBEREL MANDELA
I asked
As if in between the tears and supplication
of a mother

    Why Lord
Why are the screams of men across the whole face of the earth
Unheard
Unheeded
Unmoving
Are you one or several

Sipho Sepamla
South Africa

To the Young Mxenges

Be grieved and accept, after grief
the sorrows that life has caused you
at the hands of the government blood hounds
that mutilated your annihilated father
for no crime but the campaign to release Mandela

Be comforted after pain
of losing your last bread winner
at the hands of the castrated government eunuchs
that attacked your defenseless mother
for no crime but the defense of the motherland heroes

Be consoled my children
for there is reason to be consoled
because you have fathers and mothers
who will never forsake you
for the gullible allegation of the stupidity
of the political involvement of both your blood parents

Be resolved lastly
at this hour of your nation's destiny
to lift higher the black, the green and the gold
till the freedom charter is implemented
for none other than your own children also
our children
all children

Beaumont Sibisi
Dar-Es-Salaam, Tanzania

Let My People Go

The cold light of a winter dawn
creeps into the cell.
Opening my eyes, I this late and early breakfast and
my birthday comes to mind:
twenty-six of seventy years spent in jail;
Rivonia was but yesterday!
Soon the sun's rays
will warm my isolation,

but I will not weep,
my back will not bend
until all my people walk free.

The cold light of a winter dawn
sends shivers down my spine,
but I will not feel cold;
I am strong,
not old!
I will not submit to loneliness;
in my heart I hold you,
you fill my arms,
Africa, my people, my children.
Africa, I want, I'll own
your strong black body.
Soon it will be filled
with freedom's seed.

For my beliefs I'm in hell before death,
but I may not die,
I will not die
when you, Africa, are waiting for me!
I must not miss our meeting;
we will hold each other valiantly.
I will lead you
away from our oppressors, along
the long stormy road
to liberation.
We shall walk together,
you and I,
to our long awaited marriage,
and freedom!

Gladys Thomas
Ocean View, Cape Town
South Africa

Africa

THERE is something strange about Africa: Big letter "A"
There is something strangely large and wonderful; something
full of mystery; and something paradoxical about her history.

ANCIENT mother of the world, the earth, of man; custodian of the
missing link, the dawning Age of Cyclops, cyclone, cockatoo,
cricket, and cicada;

BEFORE monkeys were men and the bituminous, anthracitic earth
turned coal to diamonds; before carbon change and acid
test of timeless earth; before there was a Was;

BEFORE the Garden of Eden and Allah near the Nile and Tigris and
Euphrates in land between the rivers, before they harbored
the Hebraic home of the ancient Myth of Yahweh,

BEFORE Isis and Osiris were born (and the Sahara did not exist),
Africa with her mountains and plains and rain forests was
teeming Life...hot and wonderful life;

AND the races of men were cradled there...black and brown and
yellow and red. The sun baked their bread....and the hot
winds burned them to biscuit brown, to mahogany red, to
coal black blue earth from whence they came.

LIFE did not begin in the cold white frozen northern waste but
in the hot black centers of earth where the burning sands
of desert lands and hot volcanic lanes of mountain ranges
cooled with the humidity of rains.

AND the almond-eyed Orientals who slept beside the Yalu and the
Yangtse woke to call black brothers and the red-brown Orientals
who crossed Bering straits on land bridges and came to
wildernesses of forest land woke to remember their motherland
Africa-Asia and the pyramids they built were the same.

AND the Black Men in Africa rose up with spears in their hands,
   made of bone, made of stone, made of Hittite Iron and they
   became hunters of Beasts. They crossed plains and mountains
   and found antelope,

HUNTERS and shepherds grew in ancient lands where mountains spoke;
   where churning volcanoes belched smoke and rivers overflowing
   fertilized fields.

THERE is something strange about Africa; something eternal,
   more than timeless and inexplicable: how a giant sleeps;
   covering so much of all the earth; fertile and rich and
   full of wondrous things; harboring life, understanding all
   mysteries of death and time and underworlds—how a giant
   sleeps.

O Mother Earth
Dark Africa I come
to touch your sacred soil.
My ancient motherland,
Cradle of all our human lives,
Now tend these sacred fires.
Come, sacrifice your goat.
Raise altars from the myriad mountains' height
and heal our blinded sight.

How many wars and wounding battle-lines have split your body-
   earth? Cutaneous broken veins have scarred your face?
   How may times have conquerors, colonizers, slavers, soldiers
   raped you, Bosom-earth?

THE green rain-forests shed your constant tears.
   The grey mountain rocks mourn your broken heart.
   And deep desert sands take winds into your vitals.

DEEP in your bowels lie the riches of the planet earth:
   Precious stones of rubies and diamonds, of gold and silver;
   minerals' multiplicity, gurgling oil, Uranium galore, enough
   to fuel five centuries more electronic societies.

ALL fossilized energy rumbles in your belly...gas and coal and copper mines leap up and burst in prodigality.

MAGIC speaks in all your medicinal, homeopathic herbs and sympathetic nerves. Throughout our centuries of man-made time your brooding spirit covers all.

YOUR sleeping giant slumbers fitfully and mumbles in his rest against the needling gnats and flies and insects leeching him.

Wake him, Mother Africa!
Wake your sleeping giant now.
Call all your sons to destiny.
The clarion call of yet another
Age now standing in the wings
demands your keening song, your voice of humankind and kin and keenness
Awake and sing and call all your enthralled
to destiny.
Awake, Arise, thrust up your dark, burned fist
against the dawning sky.
Awake I say, stand tall.
Our dear, dark, sweet, and wondrous Africa, stand tall!

Margaret Walker

Merchants of Menace

Merchants of menace
high priests of terror
bow
to the Gods
of oppression

to drink the blood
of the poor
to quench
the thirst of the rich
a thirst
which is unquenchable

to feast from
the bodies
of the weak
and needy

capitalist cannibals
fattened
by starvation
and misery

your greed
the unborn seed
of your own death

Brian Williams
Kensington, Cape Town
South Africa

Birth Day Party

(for Nelson Mandela)

No cake
No new wish
    Years of blowing out candle fires of hate
No tightness in your belly from overeating delectables now chest now
Trunk filled w/ tuberculosis

Yet, on this 70th year
  the corners of your soul turn upward in a knowing smile
Knowing the pulse of the world drums a prelude to a real celebration,
  the Birth Day of freedom in South Africa

Freedom Band playin' for the party
  Price is high but they jam non-stop
Syncopated riffs of sighing
  soaring past high notes of suffering
Shake shake
  rattling of rock throwing warriors' dry bones
  rising to clothe themselves in freedom dust

Shriveled, humpbacked grieving Earth Mamas/Widows
    put on their last pat of powder, oils, chalk, dyes or red mud
      They swing out of their mourning clothes to Dawn
        Dawning multicolored beaded jewelry and tattered yellowed
          handmade lace of pride
      Come dance, Mamas, dance
        Dance on the moist fertile grounds of self determination
          It's party time!

Folks be comin' from all over
Your silky brown skinned queen, Warrior Winnie
  stands firm at your door
  waiting for part of her soul to return

Caribbean aunties, African uncles,
South American cousins
and North American brothers and sisters

  They be flyin', walkin', runnin', swimmin' and show-boatin'
    to the center of themselves
      to be seen at this Birth Day party

You feast on your favorite prison food
  Fried hopes dipped in corn-a-plenty batter
  Stewed dreams seasoned

w/ freshly ground Black pepper and wake-up nuts
Pit bar-b-que Botha-apartheid burning: and a full tomorrow
cooked slow and easy on scorching coals of enlightenment
havin' been basted w/ the drippings of human suffering
and rotated on a sure nuff dignified history stick

Folks be guzzlin' grapes of wrath wine
Sippin' from the fountain of
"LOVE YOUR CHILDREN BETTER THAN YOURSELF"
home brew
And savorin' Black lightnin'
100 proof positive of a prosperous future

Folks be just a sweatin'
been a laborin' a lifetime side by side
trying to plant crops in bad soil
Sweat drippin' folks
banned to a party in an imperfect world
Sweat drippin' but
determined to perfume each other
w/ the alluring sweetness of human kindness
while they slow dance to a new tune

The Birth Day gift?
The world's heart, Nelson
wrapped w/ Black, brown, yellow, white and red people
tied w/ a ribbon of melted South African gold and diamonds
An ornate package of squirming humanity on best behavior
Careful not to step on anyone's toes

Mary Ann Williams
Columbus, Ohio

89

Ukutshayelela

Xhosa Praise Poem in Pittsburghese for the Poets in Exile
(in four voices)

It is not the shields of comrades conceal you!
Nor form themselves around to extol you!
Oh, exiles bereft, only truth to console you!

hi! hi! hi!

Mighty warriors, banished from war!
Victors whose names are permitted no more!
Children, prevented your infinite wisdom!
Oh, lions, deprived of your thunderous roar!
Oh, exiled warriors, deprived of your war!

hi! hi! hi!

Singers of songs, chiding the night!
Blessing the dreamers, invoking the light!
Children, denied your brave lullabies!
Oh, Ghandis, defying saracened might!
Oh, exiled singers, defying the night!

hi! hi! hi!

Tender lovers, audacious and daring!
Only abroad hear how loved ones are faring!
Children, in desperate need of your vision!
Oh, gentle lambs, ever destined to caring!
Oh, exiled lovers, destined to daring!

hi! hi! hi!

Oh, exiled lovers, destined to daring!

hi! hi! hi!

Oh, exiled singers, defying the night!

hi! hi! hi!

Oh, exiled warriors, deprived of your war!

hi! hi! hi!

Oh, exiles bereft, it is truth must console!

hi! hi! hi!

Rachel Zepp
Pittsburgh, Pennsylvania
June 27, 1988

Places of Stone

1.
We can remember them, alone,
in their places of stone,
write heroic verse
and stirring songs,
or defer to the critics,
—art is about images,
not reporting people
chained in stone—
and leave them, alone,
to carve there
their own names (in stone)
the narcissistic horror
of being alone,
alone, alone.

2.
(for Mzwaki Mbuli)
But our brother is missing
he left his place
of refuge one day,
and went into the city
to have a beer
to sit in the sun,
watch people go by,
of Thursday
or Friday,
he had strange ways
with his days,
Wa bona? You see?
to listen
to the noises
in the street.

He walked
among the vendors
smelled the food,
touched the beads
the combs, the trinkets,
the things they sold.
He talked with friends
    "I had to come
    to the city
    to look at the people,
    I had to hear
    our comrades laugh,
    people laugh,
    I had to come,
    Wa bona? You see?"

Then our brother
went missing,
we searched
his hiding places,

"he sleeps in Mdeni
on Tuesdays,
or is it Phiri?"
Look in the places
where he looked for the people
We began
to listen
to the noises
in the street

Did they shoot him?
Already?
cut him up
blow him up
hang him up
or throw him
from a vehicle?
Did he die
as they say
     "in an unrest incident
     reported last night?"

Will we see his face,
Sad and heroic
a portrait woven
upon a T-shirt
on his burial day?
will we sing his name
     "Hamba kahle, comrade,"
shout VIVA
to his memory?

Now he seeks refuge
in our hearts,
in our memories,
in messages
engraved in stone,
in our ability
to hope-against-hope

Is he
in a dark place
somewhere,
cold and alone,
but alive?
We hope
against hope,
for our brother is missing.

3.
(for Jesse)
And this is my sister,
her face a blur
behind panes of glass,
her voice reduced to static
on an intercom.

In her home tonight
her son sits
tall and slender,
proud, and alone.
Like cold alliterations,
ice tinkling in a glass,
her name is silently
recorded, graffiti
upon the walls
of a memory
grown hard
like stones of grief.

4.
(for Eric Molobi)
A clock strikes here,
but it is not time alone
that fills the house
with a breathing sadness,
and the timelessness, here,
of waiting,

94

is filled with familiarity,
the horror has grown numb.

Eight years on an Island
was time enough to wait,
but even being alone—here—
has the certitude of choice:
Reach out, Martha,
and unbar the door,
let the cold moon
slip into your bed
like a ghostly lover.
Memory is a sad
and sordid substitute.

5.
(for one who also waited)
They came
with the usual fanfare,
screeching brakes
and the crash of doors,
and took you away,
flimsily dressed.

I watched
the fragile warmth
of our lovemaking,
wrapped around you
like a gay coat,
dissipate in the cold air,
I had nothing to offer
but silence.

I will search for you
in the labyrinth of corridors
that are to become
the days of my life,
and search for your eyes

behind the blur
of barred windows.
I will whisper
too softly
in the clamor
of visiting rooms.

I could put you
in one of my poems,
as a last resort.

6.
I have come to report
a brother is missing,
a sister taken yesterday,
a lover stolen away
as if to some unfaithful
rendezvous

let us sing heroic songs,
write unrestrained verse,
report the absence
of those who are alone,
to hell with the critics.

The alphabet,
strung together
magically creates names
that soon become
crude gougings
in the face
of indifferent stone.

A Poet of The People
South Africa

And far from the palate sea that foams beneath the suppurating syzygy of blisters, the body of my country marvelously recumbent in the despair of my arms, its bones shaking and in its veins the blood hesitating like the drop of vegetal milk at the wounded point of the bulb;

And now, suddenly, strength and life charge through me like a bull, and the wave of life surrounds the papilla of the hill, and now all the veins and capillaries swell with new blood, and the enormous, cyclonic lung breathes, and the hoarded fire of volcanoes, and the gigantic, seismic pulse beat now the measure of a living body in my firm embrace.

And we are standing now, my country and I, hair in the wind, my little hand now in its enormous fist, and the strength is not in us but above us, in a voice that pierces the night, and the audience like the sting of an apocalyptic hornet. And the voice proclaims that Europe for centuries has stuffed with lies and bloated us with pestilence,
For it is not true that the work of man is finished,
That there is nothing for us to do in this world,
That we are parasites on this earth,
That it is enough for us to keep in step with the world,
But the work of man has only just begun,
And it is up to man to vanquish all deprivations immobilized in the corners of her fervor,
And no race has the monopoly on beauty, intelligence, or strength,
And there is a place for all at the rendezvous of conquest,
And we know now that the sun turns around our earth illuminating the portion that our will alone has determined and that any star falls from sky to earth at our limitless command....

Excerpt from "Notes on a Return to the Native Land"
by Aimé Césaire
(trans. E.C.K.)

Afterword

First, we wish to thank again, all contributors to this volume: all royalties payable to poets and editors go towards an educational fund that will be established to acquire learning and teaching materials for SOMAFCO—the Solomon Mahlangu Freedom College.

This volume, we feel, amply fulfills the purposes that were initially projected: to honor Nelson Mandela in the year of his 70th birthday and give writers an opportunity to pay their tribute; to enable people of conscience to reaffirm their commitment to the struggle for Human Rights for all people; to contribute some pages to the history of the lives of some of the heroes of our time, and pay our tribute to a sterling embodiment of the strength, the endurance, and the unwavering nature of the struggle for human dignity and freedom; also to memorialize the numberless, anonymous martyrs and heroes, young and old, women and men, living and dead who are part of the enduring hope, will, dream, energy, urge, nerve, and victory.

The people shall prevail. Amandla.

It is in this spirit, then, that we next apologize to and thank the thousands who, had they known, would have contributed; even more, we express here our regret, our gratitude—to the scores of generous people who devoted time and talent to this endeavor, but whose efforts could not find space.

The work is ongoing, however, and we hope that other undertakings will be possible: the reassembling of a library for SOMAFCO; a bibliography, e.g., with Mandela as starting point—books and pamphlets like:

I Am Prepared To Die
The Struggle Is My Life
Mandela (Ronald Harwood)
Part Of My Soul Went With Him (Winnie Mandela)
For Nelson Mandela ed. Jacques Derrida and Mustapha Thili,

Seaver Books/Henry Holt, New York, 1987.
Mandela's Earth (Wole Soyinka)

In filmography: there is the documentary *Mandela*, produced by National Black Programming Consortium and Villon Films; in discography: records like *Free Nelson Mandela* by The Special AKA, Stan Campbell, Elvis Costello, and Ranking Rodger (Chrysalis Records), *African Sounds For Mandela*, by Hugh Masekela, Orchestra Jazira and Julian Bahula's *Jazz Africa* (recorded Alexandra Palace, Sunday, July 17, 1983). We can go on.

Lastly, we thank very particularly those groups, institutions, individuals, organizations, and communities that helped with stimulating, collecting, and sending contributions, that facilitated logistics, duplication, communication: there are really too many—many too many to thank, other than with a collective thank you.

However, we have to make an exception and thank by name, those four individuals whose generosity and sponsorship made it possible to get the project launched and enabled us to keep moving—in Louisville: Susan Broadhead and Jan S. Karzen, and farther away: Henry F. Wallace and Hal Wylie. We thank you all.

Hail Amandla.

Maatla